.ld b

Queen Elizabeth II

A Portrait of Britain's Monarch

by Nicholas Drummond

D0258721

Published by Trident Books Ltd.
Registered Office
506 Kingsbury Road
London NW9 9HE
www.tridentbooks.co.uk

First edition published in 2010

© 2010 Trident Books

Text copyright Nicholas Drummond

Images copyright Getty Images, the Press
Association, the National Portrait Gallery,
the Victoria and Albert Museum, the Daily Mirror,
the Royal Mint, the Bank of England and
the Royal College of Arms.

ISBN 978-0-9565568-0-6

British Cataloguing in Publication Data.
A catalogue record of this book is available
from the British Library.

Queen Elizabeth II

A Portrait of Britain's Monarch

Contents

Coronation portrait by
Sir Cecil Beaton taken
in 1953.

Introduction

Queen Elizabeth II is Head of State of the United Kingdom of Great Britain and Northern Ireland and of 15 other Commonwealth realms. Born in 1926, Her Majesty is an extraordinary person who leads an extraordinary life. Totally dedicated to the service of her people and her country, she embodies the history, customs and culture that have made Britain what it is today.

The elder daughter of King George VI (1895-1952) and Lady Elizabeth Bowes-Lyon (1900-2002), she became Queen in 1952 at the age of 25. She has reigned for more than five decades making her the United Kingdom's third longest reigning monarch and its oldest ever king or queen.

Today, Britain is a constitutional monarchy. This means that while the Queen still retains a range of executive powers, she delegates the running of the Country to a democratically elected Parliament.

Although the Queen plays no active role in the governance of the United Kingdom, after 50 years on the throne, during which time 12 Prime Ministers have served under her, she possesses considerable political and diplomatic knowledge. This makes her much more than just a ceremonial figurehead. Indeed, her wisdom and judgement have been described as indispensable national assets. Her Majesty still meets with the Prime Minister on a weekly basis. No Act of Parliament becomes law until the Queen has given it her assent.

Kings and queens have ruled Britain for more than a thousand years. In an age where so many traditions have disappeared, the British people remain committed to their Queen and to the Monarchy because they are symbols of the most enduring and successful form of government known to these shores.

The Queen has reigned for more than five decades making her the United Kingdom's third longest reigning monarch and its oldest ever king or queen.

Left: Since early Tudor times, every king and queen of the United Kingdom has had their own royal cipher or monogram. Her Majesty's cipher has the letters 'E' for Elizabeth and 'R' for Regina, which is Latin for queen. Designed by the Royal College of Heralds, it is surmounted with the St. Edward's Crown.

Birth and early life

The Queen was born on 21st April 1926. She was the first child of the Duke and Duchess of York, who later became King George VI and Queen Elizabeth, the Queen Mother. The birth took place at 17 Bruton Street in Mayfair, which was the London home of her maternal grandparents, the Earl and Countess of Strathmore.

Princess Elizabeth was a beautiful baby who charmed everyone who met her, including Winston Churchill.

At the time, King George V (1865-1936), the Queen's grandfather, was on the throne and Stanley Baldwin was Prime Minister. The Country was in the grip of an economic shutdown with the General Strike beginning a few days later.

The birth of the royal baby was a welcome relief from the prevailing gloom and generated much public interest. However, Her Royal Highness, Princess Elizabeth of York, as she was then styled, was not expected to become Queen. Preceded by her uncle, the Prince of Wales, who later became King Edward VIII (1894-1972) and her father, she was third in line to the throne.

Right: Princess Elizabeth of York with her father, King George VI and Queen Elizabeth, the Queen Mother, taken at the Princess' christening at Buckingham Palace in 1926.

Far right: Princess Elizabeth aged two years. This photograph appeared on the cover of *Time* magazine on 29th April 1929.

Princess Elizabeth with one of her parents' dogs in the garden of 145 Piccadilly, taken in 1936. Sadly, this house was destroyed by a bomb during the War after the Princess and her family had moved to Windsor.

Princess Elizabeth's grandmother, Queen Mary, described her as 'a little darling with a lovely complexion and pretty fair hair'. As early photographs show, the little Princess' blonde curls and piercing blue eyes captivated all who saw her. She was christened Elizabeth Alexandra Mary at Buckingham Palace. It was reported that she wailed throughout the service of baptism.

Although she was a princess, Elizabeth was never spoiled by excessive luxury.

Not long after her birth, Princess Elizabeth moved with her parents to a new London home at 145 Piccadilly. Although looked after by both a nanny and a governess, she was not spoiled by excessive luxury. In learning to pronounce her own name, the little Princess called herself 'Lilibet'. This became her nickname and the closest members of her family still affectionately use it today. Upon meeting Princess Elizabeth when she was barely two years old, Winston Churchill noted that 'she has an air of authority and reflectiveness astonishing in an infant'.

Princess Elizabeth riding her tricycle, circa 1930.

Portrait of the Royal Family and dogs taken in 1936 at 'Y Bwthyn Bach' (the little house in Welsh) built in the grounds of Royal Lodge, Windsor. The cottage was gift from the people of Wales and is a miniature reproduction of a typical thatched cottage from the Welsh valleys. Princess Elizabeth is behind her father, King George VI.

Facing page: Princess Elizabeth picking flowers in the garden in a picture taken by her father, King George VI, circa 1930.

This page: The future Queen on her 13th birthday riding with her father and her sister, Princess Margaret.

11

Portrait of the Royal Family wearing their coronation robes in May 1937 on the day of King George VI's coronation.

As she grew up, the young Princess spent much time in the country, including frequent trips to her grandparents' home in Scotland. This led to a love of the countryside and a lifelong interest in animals. Indeed, the Queen's abiding passion for horses began even before her grandfather, King George V, gave her a pony on her fourth birthday.

The Queen's younger sister, Margaret Rose, was born in 1930. She soon became an inseparable companion who made the long periods when their parents were away on official royal duties easier to bear. Contemporary accounts described Elizabeth as a happy, intelligent and thoughtful child while her sister, Margaret, was seen as playful and full of character. What is beyond doubt is that the family was incredibly close. King George VI said that Elizabeth was his pride and Margaret his joy.

Princess Elizabeth never expected to become Queen, just as her father had never expected to be King.

In 1936, the Queen's uncle, King Edward VIII, decided to abdicate his right to be King so that he could marry Mrs. Wallis Simpson, a divorcee. This meant that the Queen's father became King and she, under the ancient 1701 Act of Settlement, took precedence over her father's young brothers, just as Queen Victoria had taken precedence over the Duke of Cumberland, the younger brother of William IV, in 1837.

Far left: By 1932 the two princesses were already very close.

Left: The Queen with her mother, then Duchess of York, and sister in 1936, a few months before the constitutional crisis which changed their lives and destinies.

The Queen's first radio broadcast on 10th October 1940, during which she addressed the many British children who had been evacuated abroad because of the War.

Far left: Ambulance driver 2nd Lieutenant Elizabeth Windsor shortly after being commissioned into the Army's Auxiliary Territorial Reserve in 1945.

Left: Princess Elizabeth and Princess Margaret wearing their Girl Guide uniforms in 1943.

As heiress presumptive, the future Queen Elizabeth's education continued at home under her Scottish governess, Marion Crawford. She received tuition from her father, from the Vice Provost of Eton, Sir Henry Marten, and from the then Archbishop of Canterbury. She learned French from a French governess and her fluency in this language is evident today whenever official duty requires it. Princess Elizabeth also studied art and music. Together with Princess Margaret, she joined the Girl Guides and later the Sea Rangers. She became a strong swimmer, winning the Children's Challenge Shield at the London Bath Club when she was 13.

The Queen's first broadcast caught the mood of the Nation so perfectly it became a best-selling record.

When the Second World War began, Princess Elizabeth and her sister moved to Windsor Castle outside London where they stayed for the remainder of the hostilities. It was suggested that the two princesses might be safer in Canada, but their mother, Queen Elizabeth, is famously known to have said: 'The children won't go without me. I won't leave without the King. And the King will never leave'.

The Queen made her first radio broadcast in 1940 on the BBC's Children's Hour. Her message of encouragement addressed children who had been evacuated abroad: 'we children still at home are full of cheerfulness and courage. We are trying to do all we can to help our gallant sailors, soldiers and airmen, and we are trying, too, to bear our share of the danger and sadness of war. We know, every one of us, that in the end all will be well, for God will protect us and give us peace and victory. And when peace comes, it will be for us, the children of today, to make the world of tomorrow a better and happier place'. The programme proved so popular that the BBC made it into a record.

In early 1945, Princess Elizabeth joined the Women's Auxiliary Territorial Service where she trained as a driver and mechanic. The Queen is now the last surviving head of state to have served during the Second World War.

On Victory in Europe Day in 1945, Princess Elizabeth and her sister mingled anonymously with the happy crowds that thronged the streets of London. Recalling this event, she said: 'we asked my parents if we could go out and see for ourselves. We were terrified of being recognised... I remember lines of unknown people linking arms and walking down Whitehall, all of us were just swept along on a tide of happiness and relief'.

Very much a child of her times, the War years fully prepared Princess Elizabeth for her future role as Queen.

Very much a child of her times, the young Princess experienced the austerity of the Great Depression, the tragedy and uncertainty of a cataclysmic war and the great sacrifice made by so many to win it. When victory came, she was fully prepared for the manifold duties her position would subsequently demand of her.

Princess Elizabeth in 1942 by Sir Cecil Beaton. She wears the cap badge of the Grenadier Guards in her hat, having just been appointed as the Regiment's honorary Colonel.

Above: The Royal Family with the Prime Minister, Winston Churchill, wave to crowds from the balcony of Buckingham Palace in celebration of Victory in Europe, 8th May 1945.

Right: Enormous crowds of happy people in front of Buckingham Palace on VE Day 1945.

Princess Elizabeth looks over her father's shoulder as he goes through the royal boxes in his study at Windsor Castle, April 1942.

Photograph of Princess Elizabeth in 1943 taken by Yousuf Karsh.

In 1947, Princess Elizabeth made her first official overseas tour, when she accompanied her parents to South Africa. On her 21st birthday, in a radio broadcast to the British Commonwealth from South Africa, she pledged: 'I declare before you all that my whole life, whether it be long or short, shall be devoted to your service and the service of our great imperial family to which we all belong'.

After the deprivations of war, the young Princess Elizabeth became a symbol of renewal who embodied the hopes and dreams of a new generation. As public awareness of her grew, the future Queen revealed a rare aptitude for the position she would inherit. While she exuded immense strength of character and integrity, she also possessed a beauty and natural charm that made her a glamorous and appealing national icon. Eschewing film star status, a hallmark of the Windsor dynasty has been the ability to relate to ordinary people while somehow retaining the mystique of royalty.

In post-war Britain, Princess Elizabeth became a symbol of hope and renewal.

Even in her salad days, when she was green in judgement, all that Elizabeth did captured the mood of the Country perfectly, creating a surge of optimism about the future of Britain, but equally about the future of the Monarchy. There was no doubt that her accession to the throne would herald the arrival of an exciting new era.

The Royal Family during their official visit to South Africa in 1947. Princess Elizabeth is second from the right.

A radiant Queen at Buckingham Palace on the eve of her tour to India and Pakistan in January 1961.

Marriage and family

The Queen's marriage to Prince Philip is one of the greatest royal love stories. They first met as children at the wedding of the Duke of Kent in 1934, but romance did not blossom until 1939, when Princess Elizabeth and her sister accompanied their parents on a visit to the Royal Naval College at Dartmouth.

The handsome young cadet who was asked to look after the King's daughters was himself a royal prince. Prince Philip of Greece and Denmark invited the princesses to play a game of croquet. While it is almost certain that Princess Elizabeth won the game, it is not clear whether this was due to her own skill or because Prince Philip diplomatically lost. His charm and confidence clearly had an immediate effect on the Princess, but, by all accounts, the Prince himself was equally smitten.
This fateful meeting led to an exchange of letters that continued throughout the War. During his prolonged absence, the Princess kept a photograph of Prince Philip beside her bed. The official biography of King George VI, written in 1958 and approved by the Queen herself, suggests that Prince Philip was 'the man with whom Princess Elizabeth had been in love from their first meeting'.

The Queen's relationship with Prince Philip is one of the greatest royal love stories.

Prince Philip was born on the Greek Island of Corfu on 10th June 1921 and was the only son and last of five children born to Prince Andrew of Greece and Denmark and Princess Alice of Battenberg. This made him a member of the Danish-German House of Schleswig-Holstein-Sonderburg-Glücksburg, one of the most distinguished royal families of Europe. In fact, the Queen is Prince Philip's third cousin through Queen Victoria.

A delighted Princess Elizabeth with Lieutenant Philip Mountbatten shortly after announcing their engagement in 1947.

Prince Philip in the 1930s, in the classroom of the MacJannet American School in St. Cloud, Paris.

Princess Elizabeth and
the Duke of Edinburgh
at Buckingham Palace
after their wedding on
20th November 1947.

After the Greco-Turkish War, which ended in 1922, Prince Philip's parents were forced into exile. After settling in France and on the advice of his Uncle Dickie, who later became the Earl Mountbatten of Burma, Prince Philip was sent to school in England. In the absence of his parents, his uncle was a great influence on Philip. It has even been suggested that Uncle Dickie, himself a senior naval officer, arranged for his nephew to look after Princess Elizabeth at Dartmouth.

In 1933, Philip was sent to the Schloss Salem School in Germany. But, with the rise of Nazism, the school's Jewish founder, Kurt Hahn, was forced to flee from Germany to avoid persecution. Settling in Scotland, he established a new school, Gordonstoun, with Prince Philip becoming one of its first pupils.

During the Second World War, Prince Philip served with distinction in the Royal Navy. When it was over, he returned to the United Kingdom and resumed his courtship of Princess Elizabeth. Before the Prince could propose, he had to ask King George VI's permission for his daughter's hand in marriage. In order to marry the future Queen, however, Prince Philip was required to renounce his own royal titles. This he duly did and soon after the Royal Family's return from their official visit to South Africa in 1947, the Princess' engagement to Lieutenant Philip Mountbatten was announced.

While Philip was away during the War, Elizabeth kept his photograph by her bed.

Generating huge public interest, the royal couple were married at Westminster Abbey on 20th November 1947. Shortly before the wedding, Philip was created Duke of Edinburgh and granted the style of His Royal Highness by King George VI. The celebrations were not lavish since Britain was still recovering from the War. Rationing was still in force, so, like any other bride of the time, Princess Elizabeth had to collect clothing coupons to obtain the material she needed for her wedding dress. This was designed by Norman Hartnell, the superstar designer of the time. Despite the climate of restraint, the couple received more than 1,500 wedding presents from around the world.

Prince Philip's ship, HMS Valiant, in which he served in 1941.

The honeymoon was spent at Broadlands in Hampshire, which was the home of the Earl Mountbatten of Burma, and then at Birkhall on the Balmoral Estate in Scotland, where no less than six royal honeymoons have been spent.

After their wedding, the future Queen and her husband returned to live in London. Philip continued his naval career with the couple spending time in Malta. Increasingly, however, the Duke of Edinburgh began to accompany his wife on official royal duties as her Consort. When Elizabeth became Queen, she subsequently restored the titles he had renounced upon marrying her by making him a prince of the United Kingdom.

In 2007, the Queen and Prince Philip celebrated their diamond wedding anniversary.

Prince Philip has become Britain's longest-serving Consort and the oldest serving partner of a reigning monarch. The Queen and her husband celebrated their diamond wedding anniversary in 2007.

Princess Elizabeth gave birth to her first child, Prince Charles, now the Prince of Wales, on 14th November 1948. He is the heir apparent to the throne. His sister, Princess Anne, now the Princess Royal, was born in 1950. Prince Andrew, the Duke of York, was born in 1960 and Prince Edward, the Earl of Wessex, followed in 1964. Each of the Queen's children has given her two grandchildren making a total of eight.

Right: The Queen with her firstborn child, Prince Charles, shortly after his birth in November 1948.

Far right: The Queen and the Duke of Edinburgh with Prince Charles (left) and Princess Anne (right) in August 1951.

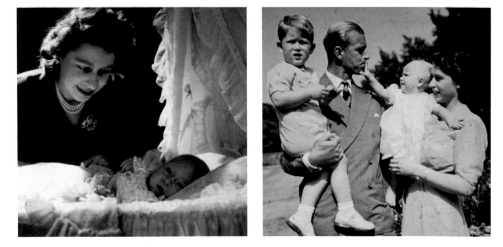

The Royal Family during their annual holiday at Balmoral in the summer of 1972. Taken by Lord Lichfield, it was one of a series of photographs used to commemorate the Queen's silver wedding anniversary. From left to right: Princess Anne, Prince Charles, Prince Edward, Prince Andrew, the Queen and the Duke of Edinburgh.

Buckingham Palace,
London.

Balmoral Castle, the
Queen's Scottish home
in Aberdeenshire.

Balmoral Castle,
Aberdeenshire

Palace of Holyroodhouse,
Edinburgh

Sandringham House,
Norfolk

Windsor Castle,
Berkshire

Buckingham Palace,
London

The Queen lives and works in a variety of magnificent royal residences where she also spends time with her family. Buckingham Palace is her official London residence. While it is a popular attraction for overseas visitors, it has for many years also been a focal point for the British people in times of celebration and crisis. Other London residences include nearby St. James's Palace, Clarence House where the Prince of Wales and the Duchess of Cornwall live with Prince William and Prince Harry, and Kensington Palace. Outside London is Windsor Castle, which is the oldest inhabited castle in the world. Sandringham House is the Queen's private home in the heart of the Norfolk countryside. The Queen's official Scottish residence is the Palace of Holyroodhouse in Edinburgh. Balmoral Castle, in Aberdeenshire, is the Queen's private Scottish home where she spends August and September.

Britain's royal residences are among the most stunning palaces and castles anywhere in the world.

Left: Windsor Castle, Berkshire.

Below left: Sandringham House, Norfolk.

Accession and coronation

King George VI had been a somewhat reluctant king and his reign placed great strains upon him. The abdication of his brother, Edward VIII, in 1937 had created a constitutional crisis. As a result, there was intense pressure on the new king to restore confidence in the Monarchy. This was followed by an even greater responsibility: being a national figurehead in a time of war when victory was far from an assured outcome before it was finally achieved in 1945. Furthermore, the sun was setting on the British Empire. As India and other colonies moved towards independence, ensuring their voluntary membership of the new Commonwealth required endless encouragement and skilful diplomacy.

The Queen's coronation heralded the arrival of a new Elizabethan age.

Sustained stress and a fondness for cigarettes led to a deterioration in the King's health. Despite the onset of cancer, King George bravely continued to fulfil as many royal duties as he could, but he increasingly relied upon Princess Elizabeth to represent him especially on overseas visits. In January 1952, King George VI unknowingly waved goodbye to his daughter for the last time as she left on a trip to Australia via Kenya. Not long afterwards, he died in his sleep at Sandringham after suffering a heart attack. The King was just 56 years old.

Right: A portrait of King George VI taken circa 1950.

Far right: King George VI lying in state at Westminster Hall in 1952 before being taken to St. George's Chapel, Windsor, for burial. Officers of the Royal Horse Guards and Life Guards and Yeoman Warders of the Tower of London, guard the coffin.

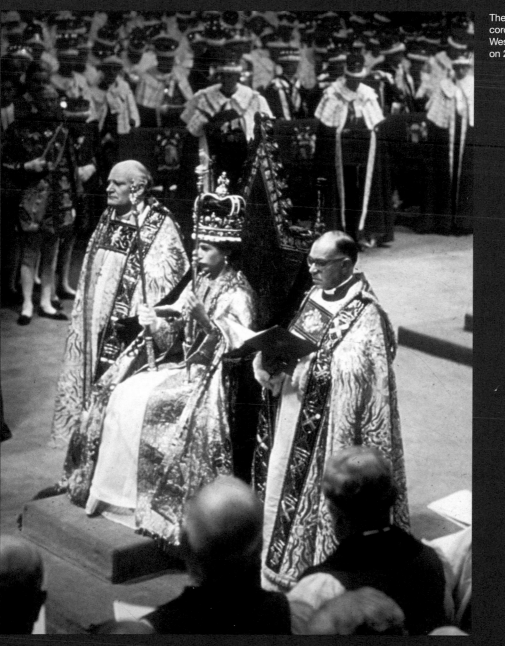

The moment of coronation at Westminster Abbey on 2nd June 1953.

The Queen smiling as she leaves Westminster Abbey after the coronation ceremony on 2nd June 1953.

Princess Elizabeth and the Duke of Edinburgh were staying at the remote Treetops hotel in Kenya at the time. It was the Duke who broke the sad news of her father's death. In order that she could be proclaimed Queen, Princess Elizabeth's private secretary, Martin Charteris, asked her what she intended to call herself as Sovereign. This was important because her father had been christened Albert, after Queen Victoria's much beloved husband, but chose to call himself King George VI. The simple and direct response to what her own title would be has come to typify our Queen: 'Elizabeth, of course'.

The royal couple's planned tour was aborted and they immediately returned to London. Thereafter, the Queen and the Duke of Edinburgh moved into what would become their primary home, Buckingham Palace. The Queen was crowned on 2nd June 1953 at Westminster Abbey. The coronation was conducted by the Archbishop of Canterbury, Dr. Geoffrey Fisher. Many distinguished guests were invited to the ceremony. They included foreign heads of state, their representatives and leading citizens from the far corners of the globe.

Far left: The *Daily Mirror* celebrates the coronation with its front page.

Left: The Queen on the cover of the coronation issue of *Picture Post* magazine, 13th June 1953.

The St. Edward's Crown is the official crown used for a coronation and its design forms the basis of all official badges of the British Monarchy, including the Queen's royal cipher. Reputed to have been made from gold originally used in the crown of Edward the Confessor (1042-1066), the Crown was remade in its current form for the coronation of Charles II in 1661. Handcrafted in 22 carat gold and set with 444 precious stones, it is the most important and valuable of the Crown Jewels.

The Queen's coronation was the first to be televised, creating a wave of interest and excitement nationally and internationally.

Weighing more than two kilos, the St. Edward's Crown is difficult to wear for long periods. After the coronation ceremony, the Queen wore the Imperial State Crown.

For the first time, and at the Queen's request, a British coronation was televised as well as being broadcast by radio. This allowed an unprecedented number of people to witness an event of great national importance. The colourful pageantry was in no way diminished by the heavy rain that fell that day with thousands of flag-waving people lining the streets and cheering in celebration of a new Elizabethan age.

The coronation was followed by royal visits to every part of the Kingdom, a review of the Navy at Spithead, and street parties in every city, town and village.

Scenes from the coronation and the celebrations that followed, 2nd June 1953.

POINT DE VUE

IMAGES DU MONDE

...VIVE LA REINE

8ᵉ ANNÉE
Nlle SÉRIE - N° 193 14 février 1952 50 fr. × EN BELGIQUE : 10 fr. belges
EN SUISSE : 0.95 suisse

The Queen's picture has been a favourite cover shot for magazines across the world since 1929. Here she is shown on the cover of French society magazine, *Point de Vue*, on her accession to the throne in 1952.

The British Monarchy

Monarchy is the oldest and most enduring form of government known to the British people. Our present sovereign can trace her roots back to William the Conqueror who invaded England in 1066. The Country has been ruled by a king or queen ever since, except from 1649 to 1660, when the Monarchy was briefly abolished following the English Civil War. Oliver Cromwell had Charles I executed and appointed himself Lord Protector of England, Scotland and Ireland, but Cromwell's republic proved to be no better than the system of monarchy it replaced. After his death, supporters of the late king restored the throne to his rightful heir, Charles II, and the Monarchy has continued to this day.

What has changed is the amount of power British monarchs have. Today, the United Kingdom is a constitutional monarchy. This is a form of government where a king or queen is head of state, but only within the boundaries of an agreed set of rules or the constitution of the state. The Sovereign's power to make new laws is delegated to a democratically elected government or Parliament. For this reason it is said that the Queen reigns but she does not rule.

The Royal Coat of Arms of the United Kingdom is the official coat of arms of the Queen and is used by her in her official capacity as Monarch.

As a constitutional monarch, the Queen still retains significant executive powers, but it is an unwritten convention that she does not exercise them. After a general election, it is she who appoints the leader of the winning party as Prime Minister and invites him or her to form a government. It is she who dissolves Parliament when a government's term in office is finished. Her Majesty is also Fount of Justice, which means that British courts derive their power from the Crown. The Queen is Commander-in-Chief of Britain's Armed Forces and Supreme Governor of the Church of England. She accredits British ambassadors and receives diplomats from foreign states.

Monarchy is the oldest and most enduring form of government known to the British people.

In theory, the Queen could unilaterally dismiss a government. In practice, she acts only on the advice of government ministers. She is politically neutral, plays no active part in the administration of the courts and no longer commands British armed forces in battle. Instead, she is a national figurehead whose duties are mostly ceremonial and symbolic.

The Queen's Speech is delivered at the State Opening of Parliament during which she outlines the Government's proposed legislative agenda.

Queen Victoria
(1819-1901) wearing
her Robes of State
in a painting
by Winterhalter.

Since the Restoration in 1660, the British Monarchy has not merely survived, but flourished due to the ability of successive kings and queens to evolve their role and responsibilities according to the will of the people. Fully accepting the importance of making appropriate changes during her own reign, the Queen became the first British monarch to pay income tax, despite the fact that historically it had always been the Crown that levied taxes.

The impact made by different British kings and queens during their reigns has seldom been measured by their power or position, but by the character and commitment they have brought to the role. Throughout her own reign, the Queen has indisputably stamped her personality on everything she has achieved. Those who know the Queen well say that she remains a very normal and down-to-earth person despite her position.

Since the Restoration in 1660, Britain's monarchy has not merely survived, but flourished.

The Royal Family is a touchstone for families everywhere. If every little girl dreams of being a princess who marries a prince, then the Queen's 60-year romance with Prince Philip helps ordinary people imagine what it would be like if such a fairytale came true. Despite the Royal Family's wealth and privilege, it has not been immune to the storms of life. The way in which the Queen's has unfailingly discharged her official duties, made personal sacrifices and her resilience is an example to us all.

King Charles II (1630-1685) by John Michael Wright, or his studio. This portrait of the King in garter robes shows him as he appeared to his subjects at the Restoration, a tall and imposing man in his thirties.

Like the first queen of hearts, her great-great-grandmother, Queen Victoria, the affection the Country feels for Elizabeth, our Queen, runs deep. Some people regard her as the mother of our nation, others as its heart. Whatever she is, the Queen is a universally respected force for good who sustains national pride and fosters a sense of community that unites an increasingly diverse kingdom.

Throughout her reign, the Queen has indisputably stamped her personality and character on everything she has achieved.

Ultimately, the value and importance of the Queen is not merely the contribution she continues to make after nearly six decades on the throne, but the fact that she has followed in the footsteps of a long line of ancestors who have each in their own way given as much as she. For all these reasons, our Monarchy is a precious symbol of stability and national identity and therefore something that the British people wish to perpetuate.

The Royal Standard is the official flag of the Sovereign of the United Kingdom. It is flown above royal palaces and castles whenever the Queen is in residence and on royal cars, ships or other vehicles whenever the Queen is travelling in them on official journeys. The four quadrants denote the ancient kingdoms of the British Isles.

The three gold lions passant guardant on a red background represent England and Wales; (Wales is a principality not a kingdom, so does not have its own heraldic design). The single red lion rampant on a gold background represents Scotland. The gold harp on a blue background represents Northern Ireland.

The Union flag, also known as the Union Jack, is the official national flag of the United Kingdom. It is flown above all official government buildings and above royal palaces and castles when the Queen is not in residence. This design has been used since the Act of Union joined England, Scotland and Ireland together as a single kingdom in 1801.

The Union flag is comprised of the three national flags of the ancient kingdoms. The cross of St. George (left) represents England; the cross of St. Andrew (middle) represents Scotland; and the cross of St. Patrick (right) represents Ireland.

The Queen reading her annual speech at the State Opening of Parliament in 2002.

44

The Queen and Prince Philip walk through the Royal Gallery at the Houses of Parliament, Westminster as she prepares to address the House of Lords and House of Commons during the State Opening of Parliament.

Royal duties

Every year, the Queen performs hundreds of official duties. Few people have a fuller diary or a more demanding schedule. Each day, the Queen will receive a number of official papers and letters that require her attention. She will be briefed on a vast range of issues affecting the United Kingdom, the Commonwealth and other areas of national interest. As a great supporter of charities, the Queen is patron or involved with more than 3,000 such organisations.

Few people have a fuller diary or a more demanding schedule than Queen Elizabeth.

One of Her Majesty's most important and colourful duties is the State Opening of Parliament. This is an annual event that usually takes place in November or December, or just after a general election when a new government assumes power, and marks the beginning of a new parliamentary session.

During the ceremony the Queen wears the Imperial State Crown. Normally, this is kept at the Tower of London where it may be seen on display in the Jewel House.

The Imperial State Crown. Originally made for George VI in 1937. It is set with more than 3,000 gemstones, including the Second Star of Africa (the second largest stone cut from the famous Cullinan diamond), the Black Prince's ruby, the Stuart sapphire, St. Edward's sapphire and Queen Elizabeth I's pearls.

Just prior to the State Opening of Parliament, the Queen may wear the Crown for a few hours each day to get used to its heavy weight. Perhaps the only time the Queen is seen wearing a crown at breakfast is when she is practising for the State Opening of Parliament.

The Queen taking the salute at Trooping the Colour in 1983 riding Burmese, the horse given to her by the Royal Canadian Mounted Police. Here she wears the uniform of the Grenadier Guards of which she is Colonel-in-Chief.

Right: Pope John Paul II exchanging gifts with the Queen when she became the first British monarch to visit the Vatican in 1980.

Below right: British coins from the Royal Mint bearing the four different versions of the Queen's portrait used during her reign.

Another important event is the weekly audience granted to the Prime Minister, during which the Queen will be briefed on parliamentary activities and other affairs of state. This usually takes place on a Tuesday evening, lasts about an hour and is entirely private.

Her Majesty regularly receives foreign heads of state and ambassadors as well as granting audiences for British political ministers and other dignitaries. During investitures, the Queen presents honours and awards to individuals in recognition of great achievement or service. She holds banquets and receptions on a wide variety of official occasions. Each year, she entertains many thousands of guests in great style and comfort.

The Queen with the First Lady of France, Carla Bruni, wife of President Nicolas Sarkozy, during his state visit to the United Kingdom in 2008.

The Queen greets
President Obama and
his wife, Michelle,
during the President's
state visit to Britain
in April, 2009.

The Queen frequently travels nationally and internationally. As well as visiting Commonwealth countries, she has been a guest of the Pope, the President of the United States and other foreign royal families. Her Majesty has opened hospitals, universities and all types of buildings. She has christened ships, opened airports, as well reviewed navies, armies and air forces.

As the Commander-in-Chief of Britain's Armed Forces, the Queen has close ties with all three services with many serving officers seconded from their units or regiments to help fulfil her many duties. Each year, on the occasion of her official birthday, Her Majesty takes the salute at Trooping the Colour. Participating in this parade are soldiers from the seven Guards regiments, who have been the Sovereign's official bodyguards for more than 300 years.

Despite reaching an age when most grandmothers relax and enjoy the freedom of retirement, Her Majesty remains as busy as ever. In 2009, she conducted more than 300 royal engagements.

Far left: The Queen makes a speech at a state banquet held at Windsor Castle.

Left: The Queen bestows a knighthood during an investiture at Buckingham Palace.

The Queen returns to
Buckingham Palace
after the Trooping the
Colour ceremony.

The Queen and the Commonwealth

President Mandela of
South Africa rides in
the Queen's carriage
during his state visit in
July 1996.

The Commonwealth is an international organisation comprised of 53 independent member states, including the United Kingdom. Many, but not all, were formerly part of the British Empire. Established in 1949 as the Commonwealth of Nations, it is not a political union but a community of states operating under a set of shared values to achieve common social, cultural and economic goals. The most important of these are democracy, freedom and peace. Perhaps the best description of the Commonwealth is the Queen's own: 'It's a rather special family, a family of nations'.

The Commonwealth is a community of states with shared values and common goals.

The Queen is the Head of Commonwealth. As such, her role and powers are very similar to those she has as Head of State of the United Kingdom, but she never exercises them. Instead, it is the personal relationships that Her Majesty has built with the leaders of Commonwealth member states that have been the foundation of its success.

In addition to being the Queen of the United Kingdom of Great Britain and Northern Ireland, Her Majesty is also the Queen of 15 other independent Commonwealth realms: Antigua and Barbuda, Australia, the Bahamas, Barbados, Belize, Canada, Grenada, Jamaica, New Zealand, Papua New Guinea, St. Kitts and Nevis, St. Lucia, St. Vincent and the Grenadines, the Solomon Islands and Tuvalu. All of these countries are constitutional monarchies. Were the Queen ever to cease to be the Queen of the United Kingdom, it is quite possible that she could continue to be Queen of any, if not all, of the Commonwealth realms.

Above:
The Commonwealth flag. The design incorporates a globe encircled with 61 radiating spears that form the letter 'C'. These do not represent the number of countries in the Commonwealth, but symbolise the many ways in which member states co-operate around the world.

Left: Flags of the Commonwealth realms.

Antigua & Barbuda

Australia

The Bahamas

Barbados

Belize

Canada

Grenada

Jamaica

New Zealand

Papua New Guinea

St. Kitts & Nevis

St. Lucia

St. Vincent and the Grenadines

The Solomon Islands

Tuvalu

Right: The Queen launches the 2010 Commonwealth Games, due to take place in New Delhi, by passing the baton to India's president, Pratibha Patil, during a state visit to London. The baton will travel the length and breadth of the Commonwealth.

Far right: When visiting Commonwealth member states that are not Commonwealth realms, the Queen uses her personal flag instead of the Royal Standard. The design is based on a simplified royal cipher surrounded by roses to represent Commonwealth member states. It was first used during Her Majesty's state visit to India in 1961.

Commonwealth member states that are not Commonwealth realms have separate heads of state. Of the total, 32 are republics with presidents including: Bangladesh, Botswana, Cameroon, Cyprus, Dominica, the Fiji Islands, the Gambia, Ghana, Grenada, Guyana, India, Kenya, Kiribati, Malawi, the Maldives, Malta, Mauritius, Mozambique, Namibia, Nauru, Nigeria, Pakistan, Samoa, the Seychelles, Sierra Leone, Singapore, South Africa, Sri Lanka, Uganda, Tanzania, Vanuatu and Zambia. Five have their own monarchs: Brunei Darussalam, Lesotho, Malaysia, Swaziland and Tonga.

One of the most significant achievements of the Queen's reign has been to build the Commonwealth beyond being simply a collection of former British colonies. Mozambique, for example, has no direct link to the United Kingdom, because it was a Portuguese colony not a British one. From time to time, the membership of various states has been suspended, such as South Africa, when it had a policy of apartheid, and the Fiji Islands, when its democratic government was overthrown by a military coup.

In 2009, the Commonwealth celebrated its 60th anniversary. The mutual support that Commonwealth member states continue to provide to each other, including aid in times of crisis, educational initiatives, trade agreements, investment and other economic benefits, has created a model of international co-operation that has won the respect and admiration of people everywhere. Few other international organisations have achieved greater unity among their members.

The Commonwealth is a model of international co-operation and has achieved an unparalleled unity among its members.

The Queen being
carried down the main
street of Tuvalu, in the
South Pacific, in a war
canoe.

The Royal Family today

Although the Queen's public life is full and unremitting, making time for her family has always been a priority. When not involved in public engagements, there is nothing Her Majesty likes more than inviting her children and grandchildren to stay.

As the Queen's eldest child, Prince Charles, now Prince of Wales, is heir apparent to the throne. After studying at Trinity College, Cambridge, the Prince followed the family tradition of joining the Royal Navy. He is also a qualified pilot and parachutist and has strong links with the Army and Royal Air Force. Since leaving the Navy, Prince Charles has become well known for his charity work, establishing among other foundations the Prince's Trust in 1976 to help disadvantaged young people.

The Queen's commitment to her country is only matched by her love for her family.

As someone concerned about the environment, the Prince has been a champion of the natural world, urban renewal and organic farming. Following in the footsteps of his ancestors, who built some of the Country's most important and iconic buildings, it is no surprise that the Prince also takes a great interest in architecture. He cares deeply about the impact of buildings, both on individuals, and on the communities in which they are built.

Prince Charles, the Prince of Wales, photographed wearing the uniform of the Welsh Guards on his 60th birthday.

The Prince performs a wide variety of royal engagements and increasingly represents his mother in addition to fulfilling his own official duties.

The Royal Family on the balcony of Buckingham Palace. From left to right: Princess Beatrice, the Duke of York, Princess Eugenie, Prince William, the Queen, the Duchess of Cornwall the Duke of Edinburgh, the Prince of Wales, Viscount Linley, the Princess Royal.

The Prince of Wales
holds Prince Harry
while Diana, the
Princess of Wales,
holds Prince William
at their home
Highgrove House
in Gloucestershire
in 1986.

Left: Prince William enjoys a joke with his father during a skiing holiday in Klosters 2004.

Below left: Both Prince William and Prince Harry have followed the royal tradition of serving in Britain's armed forces. They are pictured here during their training at the Defence Helicopter Flying School, RAF Shawbury.

The Prince of Wales married Lady Diana Spencer in 1981. They had two boys, Prince William and Prince Harry. Since their mother's tragic death in 1997, the two princes have become particularly close to their grandmother. The Prince of Wales is now married to Camilla, the Duchess of Cornwall.

Prince William and Prince Harry were both educated at Eton College, near Windsor. After studying for a degree at St. Andrew's University, Prince William joined the Army. He subsequently transferred to the Royal Air Force and has gained his pilot's wings. Prince William will succeed his father and, as second in line to the throne, has begun to carry out official duties, including some on behalf of his grandmother.

Prince Harry, who is a keen sportsman, also joined the Army. When he served with his regiment, the Blues and Royals, in Afghanistan in 2007, he became the first member of the Royal Family to serve in a war zone since his uncle, Prince Andrew, served as a Royal Navy helicopter pilot during the Falklands War in 1982.

Princess Anne, the Princess Royal, is the Queen's second child and only daughter. Like her mother, Princess Anne is an accomplished horsewoman. She has competed internationally winning many medals and prizes. The Princess was a member of the British Equestrian team at the 1976 Olympic games when she rode Goodwill, a horse owned by the Queen. Through her marriage to Captain Mark Phillips, the Princess Royal has two children, Peter Phillips and Zara Phillips. The Princess is now married to Vice-Admiral Timothy Lawrence. Peter Phillips was the first of the Queen's grandchildren to marry when he wed Autumn Kelly in 2008. The Queen's granddaughter, Zara Phillips, is also a horsewoman of international renown and became the Eventing World Champion at the World Equestrian Games in 2006.

Prince Andrew, the Duke of York, enjoyed a successful career spanning 22 years in the Royal Navy where he served as a helicopter pilot. He is now the United Kingdom's Special Representative for International Trade and Investment. Prince Andrew has two daughters through his marriage to Sarah Ferguson, Princess Beatrice and Princess Eugenie. The Prince is a keen golfer.

Prince Edward, the Earl of Wessex, is involved with a number of charities and organisations. Prince Edward has a daughter and a son through his marriage to Sophie Rhys-Jones, Louise and James, Viscount Severn. The Prince is a great supporter of the Arts.

Right: Princess Anne, the Princess Royal, photographed at the Royal Wedding in 1981.

Centre right: Prince Andrew, the Duke of York.

Far right: Prince Edward, the Earl of Wessex and Sophie, the Countess of Wessex, with their first child, Lady Louise Windsor.

Three generations
of the Royal Family
celebrate the 50th
anniversary of the
Queen's coronation
in June 2003.

The Queen arriving
at Royal Ascot
in June 2004.

Interesting facts about the Queen

The Queen is a great animal lover and breeds both horses and dogs. She learnt to ride at an early age and has a great knowledge of all things equestrian. Each year Her Majesty attends the Derby at Epsom and Royal Ascot, two highlights of the flat racing calendar, which she enjoys very much. Her Majesty's racehorses frequently participate. Over the years, her horses have won many trophies.

The Queen's abiding passion for horses began even before her grandfather, King George V, gave her a pony on her fourth birthday.

The Queen also breeds working labradors at Sandringham, her country home in Norfolk. On her 18th birthday, the Queen was given a corgi puppy by her parents. Called Susan, this dog was the first in a long line of much loved pets. Today, the Queen has eight dogs; four are corgis directly descended from her first one and are called Linnet, Holly, Willow and Monty. The Queen also has four dorgis (the name given to a crossbreed of corgis and dachshunds) and their names are Cider, Berry, Candy and Vulcan.

Giving new meaning to the term 'royal portrait', the Queen enjoys being on the other side of the camera lens.

The Queen riding with
President Ronald
Reagan in Windsor
Great Park during his
state visit to Britain in
June 1982.

Right: The Queen is clearly amused as local corgi enthusiasts in Edmonton, Alberta greet her during her state visit to Canada in 2005.

Below right: The one pound bank note, now withdrawn from circulation, was the first British banknote to carry a portrait of the Monarch. Designed by Robert Austin it was first issued in 1960.

The Queen and the Prince of Wales enjoying the Highland games at the 2006 Braemar Gathering in Scotland.

The Queen is extremely fond of Scotland having spent many of her most formative years in the Highlands. She adores the countryside and outdoor pursuits. The Queen also enjoys Scottish dancing to the sound of the bagpipes and hosts regular dances when staying at Balmoral.

A little-known fact about the Queen is that she has a great sense of humour. It is rumoured that she enjoys playing the after-dinner game, charades, where players divide into two teams and have to act out the names of famous people, books or films. By all accounts, the Queen is very good and makes her guests roar with laughter. The Queen is a keen photographer and besides taking pictures of her family, is reputed to have a good eye for landscape shots and animals portraits.

A little-known fact about the Queen is that she has a great sense of humour.

Timeline of key events during the Queen's life

1926 – Princess Elizabeth Alexandra Mary of York born on 21st April, two weeks before the General Strike. The Queen's grandfather, George V, is the King.

1929 – The Wall Street Crash. First transmission of John Logie Baird's 30-line television. First telephone boxes appear in London.

1930 – Princess Margaret Rose, the Queen's sister is born. Dwarf planet Pluto discovered by US astronomers.

1936 – George V dies. Edward VIII creates constitutional crisis and abdicates to marry Mrs. Wallis Simpson. The Queen's father becomes George VI. RMS Queen Mary begins transatlantic service.

1939 – Britain declares war on Nazi Germany. Princess Elizabeth and her sister are evacuated to Windsor.

1940 – Winston Churchill becomes Prime Minister. Princess Elizabeth makes her first radio broadcast on BBC's Children's Hour.

1945 – Princess Elizabeth joins the Army as an ambulance driver. Victory in Europe. Clement Atlee becomes Prime Minister. United Nations established.

1947 – Princess Elizabeth makes first overseas tour. Engagement to Lieutenant Philip Mountbatten followed by marriage at Westminster Abbey.

1948 – Birth of Prince Charles. London hosts the Olympic Games.

1949 – The Commonwealth is established.
NATO alliance formed.

1950 – Birth of Princess Anne. First motor racing Grand Prix
held at Silverstone. Korean War starts.

1952 – King George VI dies. Maiden flight of the first jet
powered passenger aircraft, the Comet.

1953 – Coronation of Elizabeth II. Mount Everest conquered
by Sir Edmund Hillary and Sherpa Tensing. Ian Fleming
publishes first James Bond novel.

1957 – Queen's annual Christmas message is broadcast
on television for the first time. Russians launch Sputnik 1,
the first satellite to orbit the earth.

1960 – Prince Andrew is born. Princess Margaret,
the Queen's sister, marries Anthony Armstrong-Jones.

1963 – President Kennedy assassinated. The Beatles release
their first number one hit record *Please Please Me.*

1964 – Prince Edward is born. Nelson Mandela sentenced
to life imprisonment.

1966 – England win the football World Cup. State Opening
of Parliament televised for the first time.

1969 – Prince Charles' investiture as the Prince of Wales.
Neil Armstrong and Buzz Aldrin become the first human
beings to set foot on the moon.

1972 – Duke of Windsor dies. First hand-held calculator introduced.

1973 – Princess Anne marries Captain Mark Phillips. Watergate scandal in the USA.

1977 – The Queen celebrates her Silver Jubilee – 25 years on the throne. Princess Anne and Mark Phillips have a son, Peter Phillips, the Queen's first grandchild.

1979 – The Duke of Edinburgh's uncle, Lord Mountbatten, killed by an IRA bomb. Margaret Thatcher becomes the UK's first woman Prime Minister.

1980 – The Queen becomes first British monarch to make a state visit to the Vatican.

1981 – Prince Charles marries Lady Diana Spencer. Princess Anne and Mark Phillips have a daughter, Zara Phillips. IBM introduces first personal computer.

1982 – Falklands War during which Prince Andrew is a helicopter pilot for the Royal Navy. Prince William is born and becomes second in line to the throne.

1984 – Prince Harry is born and becomes third in line to the throne.

1986 – The Queen celebrates her 60th birthday. Becomes the first British Monarch to visit China. Duchess of Windsor, Wallis Simpson, dies. Prince Andrew marries Sarah Ferguson.

1988 – Prince Andrew and the Duchess of York have a daughter, Princess Beatrice.

1989 – President Gorbachev of the USSR visits the Queen. Berlin Wall torn down.

1990 – Prince Andrew and the Duchess of York have a second daughter, Princess Eugenie. Nelson Mandela released from prison.

1992 – Fire severely damages Windsor Castle.

1993 – The Queen starts to pay income tax to the Inland Revenue.

1997 – The Queen and Duke of Edinburgh celebrate their 50th wedding anniversary. Princess Diana dies in a car crash.

1999 – Prince Edward, Earl of Wessex, marries Sophie Rhys-Jones.

2002 – The Queen celebrates her Golden Jubilee – 50 years on the throne. The Queen's younger sister Princess Margaret dies after a long illness. The Queen Mother dies aged 101.

2003 – Prince Edward and the Countess of Wessex have a daughter, Lady Louise Windsor.

2005 – Prince Charles marries Camilla Parker-Bowles, who becomes the Duchess of Cornwall.

2006 – The Queen celebrates her 80th birthday.

2007 – The Queen and Duke of Edinburgh celebrate their 60th wedding anniversary. Becomes the United Kingdom's oldest serving monarch, surpassing the record held by Queen Victoria. Prince Edward and the Countess of Wessex have a son, James, Viscount Severn.

2008 – Prince Charles' 60th birthday.

2009 – The Commonwealth's 60th anniversary.

2010 – The Queen celebrates her 84th birthday.

The Queen at
Horseguards Parade
in London during the
Trooping the Colour
ceremony in June 1972.
She wears a black
armband, the symbol
of court mourning, after
the death of her uncle,
the Duke of Windsor.

English kings and queens since 1066

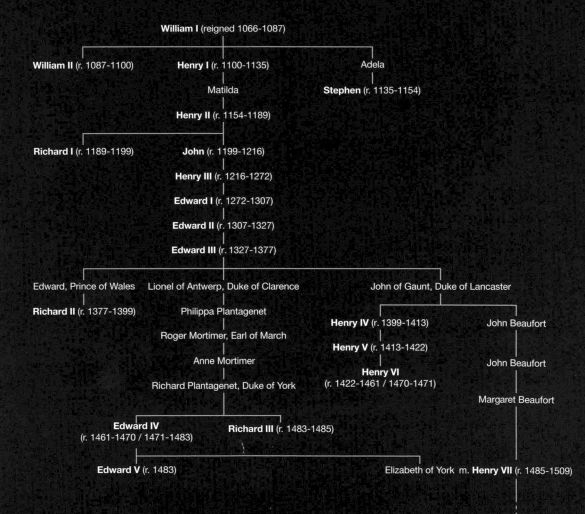

William I (reigned 1066-1087)

William II (r. 1087-1100)   **Henry I** (r. 1100-1135)   Adela

Matilda   **Stephen** (r. 1135-1154)

Henry II (r. 1154-1189)

Richard I (r. 1189-1199)   **John** (r. 1199-1216)

Henry III (r. 1216-1272)

Edward I (r. 1272-1307)

Edward II (r. 1307-1327)

Edward III (r. 1327-1377)

Edward, Prince of Wales   Lionel of Antwerp, Duke of Clarence   John of Gaunt, Duke of Lancaster

Richard II (r. 1377-1399)   Philippa Plantagenet   **Henry IV** (r. 1399-1413)   John Beaufort

Roger Mortimer, Earl of March   **Henry V** (r. 1413-1422)

Anne Mortimer   **Henry VI**   John Beaufort
(r. 1422-1461 / 1470-1471)

Richard Plantagenet, Duke of York   Margaret Beaufort

Edward IV   **Richard III** (r. 1483-1485)
(r. 1461-1470 / 1471-1483)

Edward V (r. 1483)   Elizabeth of York m. **Henry VII** (r. 1485-1509)

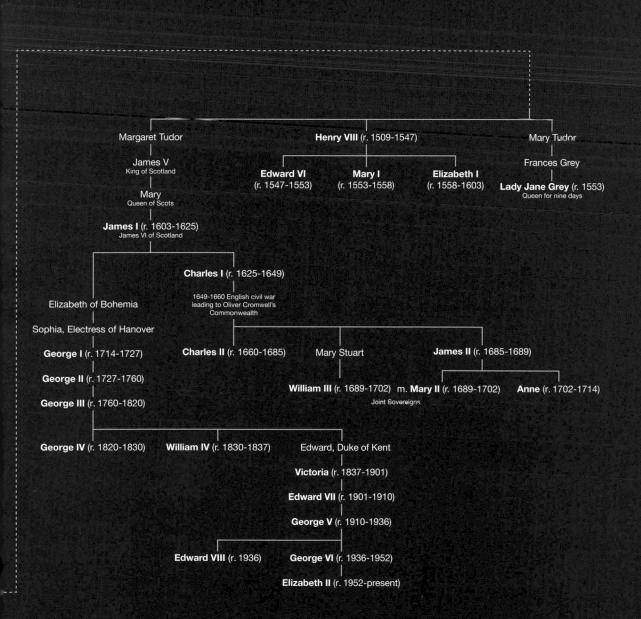

Margaret Tudor

Henry VIII (r. 1509-1547)

Mary Tudor

James V
King of Scotland

Edward VI
(r. 1547-1553)

Mary I
(r. 1553-1558)

Elizabeth I
(r. 1558-1603)

Frances Grey

Lady Jane Grey (r. 1553)
Queen for nine days

Mary
Queen of Scots

James I (r. 1603-1625)
James VI of Scotland

Charles I (r. 1625-1649)

1649-1660 English civil war
leading to Oliver Cromwell's
Commonwealth

Elizabeth of Bohemia

Sophia, Electress of Hanover

George I (r. 1714-1727)

Charles II (r. 1660-1685)

Mary Stuart

James II (r. 1685-1689)

George II (r. 1727-1760)

William III (r. 1689-1702)

m. **Mary II** (r. 1689-1702)

Anne (r. 1702-1714)

Joint Sovereigns

George III (r. 1760-1820)

George IV (r. 1820-1830)

William IV (r. 1830-1837)

Edward, Duke of Kent

Victoria (r. 1837-1901)

Edward VII (r. 1901-1910)

George V (r. 1910-1936)

Edward VIII (r. 1936)

George VI (r. 1936-1952)

Elizabeth II (r. 1952-present)

British National Anthem

God save our gracious Queen,
Long live our noble Queen,
God save the Queen:
Send her victorious,
Happy and glorious,
Long to reign over us:
God save the Queen.

O Lord, our God, arise,
Scatter her enemies,
And make them fall.
Confound their politics,
Frustrate their knavish tricks,
On Thee our hopes we fix,
God save us all.

Thy choicest gifts in store,
On her be pleased to pour;
Long may she reign:
May she defend our laws,
And ever give us cause
To sing with heart and voice
God save the Queen.

Portrait of the Queen by Italian artist, Pietro Annigoni, painted in 1954.

About the author

Nicholas Drummond is a writer and strategy consultant who runs his own marketing advisory firm. He spent six years in the Welsh Guards, during which time he developed a unique knowledge of and affection for Britain's Royal Family. He read Law and Economics at Trinity College, Cambridge and attended the Royal Military Academy, Sandhurst. He lives in London with his wife and three children.

Acknowledgements

The author would like to thank the following for their help and advice in writing this book: the Royal College of Arms, the Royal Mint, the Bank of England, Getty Images, the Press Association, the Daily Mirror, the Victoria and Albert Museum, the National Portrait Gallery, the official website of the British Monarchy at www.royal.gov.uk

Front cover images from left to right:

Princess Elizabeth with one of the family's corgis at her home at 145 Piccadilly, London, 1936.

Official portrait of Princess Elizabeth taken by Yousuf Karsh in 1951.

The Queen visits the Royal Horticultural Society Garden at Wisley, Surrey, 2004.

Back cover images from left to right:

The Queen in 1952, the year she acceded to the throne.

The Queen and the Duke of Edinburgh celebrating their diamond wedding anniversary in 2007 at Broadlands, the Mountbatten family home, where they had spent their honeymoon.

Inside covers

Royal Stewart tartan, the personal tartan of Queen Elizabeth II.

CarbonNeutral.com
CO₂ emissions reduced to net zero in accordance with The CarbonNeutral Protocol